William Chambers

A Dissertation on Oriental Gardening

William Chambers

A Dissertation on Oriental Gardening

ISBN/EAN: 9783337090869

Printed in Europe, USA, Canada, Australia, Japan

Cover: Foto ©Thomas Meinert / pixelio.de

More available books at **www.hansebooks.com**

DISSERTATION
ON
ORIENTAL GARDENING,
BY
Sᴿ WILLIAM CHAMBERS, Kɴᵗ.
Comptroller General of his Majesty's Works.

LONDON:

Printed by W. GRIFFIN, Printer to the ROYAL ACADEMY; fold by Him in *Catherine street;* and by T. DAVIES, Bookfeller to the ROYAL ACADEMY, in *Ruffel street, Covent Garden;* alſo by J. DODSLEY, *Pall Mall;* WILSON and NICOLL, *Strand;* J. WALTER *Charing Croſs;* and P. ELMSLEY, *Strand.* 1772.

TO
THE KING.

I HUMBLY beg leave to lay at Your MAJESTY's feet the following Differtation upon an Art of which You are the firft Judge, as well as the moft munificent Encourager.

A Sketch of the prefent little Performance was gracioufly received by Your MAJESTY many years ago, and found a kind reception in the world, under the Influence of Your Patronage. This is more ample, I wifh it may be more perfect than the original; that it may have a jufter title to Your Indulgence, and better pretenfions to the favor of the Publick.
I am,

        May it pleafe Your MAJESTY.
          Your MAJESTY's
      dutiful fervant and faithful fubject,

WILLIAM CHAMBERS.

PREFACE.

AMONGST the decorative arts, there is none of which the influence is so extensive as that of Gardening. The productions of other arts have their separate classes of admirers, who alone relish or set any great value upon them; to the rest of the world they are indifferent, sometimes disgusting. A building affords no pleasure to the generality of men, but what results from the grandeur of the object, or the value of its materials: nor doth a picture affect them, but by its resemblance to life. A thousand other beauties, of a higher kind, are lost upon them; for in Architecture, in Painting, and indeed in most other arts, men must learn before they can admire: their pleasure keeps pace with their judgment; and it is only by knowing much, that they can be highly delighted.

But Gardening is of a different nature: its dominion is general; its effects upon the human mind certain and invariable; without any previous information, without being taught, all men are delighted with the gay luxuriant scenery of summer, and depressed at the dismal aspect of autumnal prospects; the charms of cultivation are equally sensible to the ignorant and the learned, and they are equally disgusted at the rudeness of neglected nature; lawns, woods, shrubberies, rivers and mountains, affect them both in the same manner; and every combination of these will excite similar sensations in the minds of both.

Nor are the productions of this Art less permanent than general in their effects. Pictures, statues, buildings, soon glut the sight, and grow indifferent to the spectator: but in gardens there is a continual state of fluctuation, that leaves no room for satiety; the progress of vegetation, the vicissitudes of seasons, the changes of the weather, the different directions of the sun, the passage of clouds, the agitation and sounds produced by winds,

together

PREFACE. iii

together with the accidental intervention of living or moving objects, vary the appearances so often, and so considerably, that it is almost impossible to be cloyed, even with the same prospects.

Is it not singular then, that an Art with which a considerable part of our enjoyments is so universally connected, should have no regular professors in our quarter of the world? Upon the continent it is a collateral branch of the architect's employment, who, immersed in the study and avocations of his own profession, finds no leisure for other disquisitions; and, in this island, it is abandoned to kitchen gardeners, well skilled in the culture of sallads, but little acquainted with the principles of Ornamental Gardening. It cannot be expected that men uneducated, and doomed by their condition to waste the vigor of life in hard labour, should ever go far in so refined, so difficult a pursuit.

To this unaccountable want of regular masters may, in a great measure, be ascribed the scarcity of perfect gardens.

gardens. There are indeed very few in our part of the globe wherein nature has been improved to the best advantage, or art employed with the soundest judgment. The gardens of Italy, France, Germany, Spain, and of all the other countries where the antient style still prevails, are in general mere cities of verdure; the walks are like streets conducted in strait lines, regularly diverging from different large open spaces, resembling public squares; and the hedges with which they are bordered, are raised, in imitation of walls, adorned with pilasters, niches, windows and doors, or cut into colonades, arcades and porticos; all the detached trees are shaped into obelisks, pyramids and vases; and all the recesses in the thickets bear the names and forms of theatres, amphitheatres, temples, banqueting halls, ball rooms, cabinets and saloons. The streets and squares are well manned with statues of marble or lead, ranged in regular lines, like soldiers at a procession; which, to make them more natural, are sometimes painted in proper colours, and finely gilt. The lakes and rivers are confined by quais of hewn stone, and taught to flow in geometrick order;

and the cafcades glide from the heights by many a fucceffion of marble fteps: not a twig is fuffered to grow as nature directs; nor is a form admitted but what is fcientific, and determinable by the line or compafs.

In England, where this antient ftyle is held in deteftation, and where, in oppofition to the reft of Europe, a new manner is univerfally adopted, in which no appearance of art is tolerated, our gardens differ very little from common fields, fo clofely is common nature copied in moft of them; there is generally fo little variety in the objects, fuch a poverty of imagination in the contrivance, and of art in the arrangement, that thefe compofitions rather appear the offspring of chance than defign; and a ftranger is often at a lofs to know whether he be walking in a meadow, or in a pleafure ground, made and kept at a very confiderable expence: he fees nothing to amufe him, nothing to excite his curiofity, nor any thing to keep up his attention. At his firft entrance, he is treated with the fight of a large green field, fcattered over with a few ftraggling trees, and verged with a confufed border forming either; and consequently prejudice himself, without doing service to the Art.

But though it might be impertinent as well as useless to start a new system of one's own, it cannot be improper, nor totally unserviceable, to publish that of others; especially of a people whose skill in Gardening has often been the subject of praise; and whose manner has been set up amongst us as the standard of imitation, without ever having been properly defined. It is a common saying, That from the worst things some good may be extracted; and even if what I have to relate should be inferior to what is already known, yet surely some useful hints may be collected from it.

I may therefore, without danger to myself, and it is hoped without offence to others, offer the following account of the Chinese manner of Gardening; which is collected from my own observations in China, from conversations with their Artists, and remarks transmitted to me at different times by travellers. A sketch of what I have

P R E F A. C E.

I have now attempted to finish, was published some years ago; and the favourable reception granted to that little performance, induced me to collect materials for this.

Whether the Chinese manner of Gardening be better or worse than those now in use amongst the Europeans, I will not determine: comparison is the surest as well as the easiest test of truth; it is in every man's power to compare and to judge for himself.---Should the present publication contain any thing useful, my purpose will be fully answered; if not, it may perhaps afford some little entertainment, or serve at worst to kill an idle hour.

I must not enter upon my subject, without apologizing for the liberties here taken with our English Gardens: there are, indeed, several that do not come within the compass of my description; some of which were laid out by their owners, who are as eminently skilled in Gardening, as in many other branches of polite knowledge; the rest owe most of their excellence to nature, and are, upon the whole, very little improved by the interpofition of art; which, though it may have heightened fome of their beauties, has totally robbed them of many others.

It would be tedious to enumerate all the errors of a falfe tafte: but the havock it has made in our old plantations, muft ever be remembered with indignation: the ax has often, in one day, laid wafte the growth of feveral ages; and thoufands of venerable plants, whole woods of them, have been fwept away, to make room for a little grafs, and a few American weeds. Our virtuofi have fcarcely left an acre of fhade, nor three trees growing in a line, from the Land's-end to the Tweed; and if their humour for devaftation continues to rage much longer, there will not be a foreft-tree left ftanding in the whole kingdom.

DISSERTATION.

Amongst the Chinese, Gardening is held in much higher esteem, than it is in Europe; they rank a perfect work in that Art, with the great productions of the human understanding; and say, that its efficacy in moving the passions, yields to that of few other arts whatever.

Their Gardeners are not only Botanists, but also Painters and Philosophers, having a thorough knowledge of the human mind, and of the arts by which its strongest feelings are excited. It is not in China, as in Italy and France, where every petty Architect is a Gardener; neither is it as in another famous country, where peasants emerge from the melon grounds to commence professors; so Sganarelle, the faggot-maker, laid down his hatchet to turn physician. In China, Gardening is a distinct profession, requiring an extensive study; to the

perfection

perfection of which few arrive. The Gardeners there, far from being either ignorant or illiterate, are men of high abilities, who join to good natural parts, moſt ornaments that ſtudy, travelling, and long experience can ſupply them with: it is in conſideration of theſe accompliſhments only that they are permitted to exerciſe their profeſſion; for with the Chineſe the taſte of Ornamental Gardening is an object of legiſlative attention, it being ſuppoſed to have an influence upon the general culture, and conſequently upon the beauty of the whole country. They obſerve, that miſtakes committed in this Art, are too important to be tolerated, being much expoſed to view, and in a great meaſure irreparable; as it often requires the ſpace of a century, to redreſs the blunders of an hour.

The Chineſe Gardeners take nature for their pattern; and their aim is to imitate all her beautiful irregularities. Their firſt conſideration is the nature of the ground they are to work upon: whether it be flat or ſloping; hilly or mountainous; ſmall or of conſiderable extent; abounding

ing with springs and rivers, or labouring under a scarcity of water; whether woody or bare, rough or even, barren or rich; and whether the transitions be sudden, and the character grand, wild or tremendous; or whether they be gradual, and the general bent placid, gloomy or chearful. To all which circumstances they carefully attend; choosing such dispositions as humour the ground, hide its defects, improve or set off its advantages, and can be executed with expedition, at a moderate expence.

They are also attentive to the wealth or indigence of the patron by whom they are employed; to his age, his infirmities, temper, amusements, connections, business and manner of living; as likewise to the season of the year in which the Garden is likely to be most frequented by him: suiting themselves in their composition to his circumstances, and providing for his wants and recreations. Their skill consists in struggling with the imperfections and defects of nature, and with every other impediment; and in producing, in spite of every obstacle, works that are uncommon, and perfect in their kind.

Though the Chinese artists have nature for their general model, yet are they not so attached to her as to exclude all appearance of art; on the contrary, they think it, on many occasions, necessary to make an ostentatious shew of their labour. Nature, say they, affords us but few materials to work with. Plants, ground and water, are her only productions: and though both the forms and arrangements of these may be varied to an incredible degree, yet have they but few striking varieties, the rest being of the nature of changes rung upon bells, which, though in reality different, still produce the same uniform kind of jingling; the variation being too minute to be easily perceived.

Art must therefore supply the scantiness of nature; and not only be employed to produce variety, but also novelty and effect: for the simple arrangements of nature are met with in every common field, to a certain degree of perfection; and are therefore too familiar to excite any strong sensations in the mind of the beholder, or to produce any uncommon degree of pleasure.

It

It is indeed true that novelty and variety may both be attained by transplanting the peculiarities of one country to another; by introducing rocks, cataracts, impending woods, and other parts of romantic situations, in flat places; by employing much water where it is rare; and cultivated plains, amidst the rude irregularities of mountains: but even this resource is easily exhausted, and can seldom be put in practice, without a very great expence.

The Chinese are therefore no enemies to strait lines; because they are, generally speaking, productive of grandeur, which often cannot be attained without them: nor have they any aversion to regular geometrical figures, which they say are beautiful in themselves, and well suited to small compositions, where the luxuriant irregularities of nature would fill up and embarrass the parts they should adorn. They likewise think them properest for flower gardens, and all other compositions, where much art is apparent in the culture; and where it should therefore not be omitted in the form.

Their

Their regular buildings they generally surround with artificial terrasses, slopes, and many flights of steps; the angles of which are adorned with groupes of sculpture and vases, intermixed with all sorts of artificial waterworks, which, connecting with the architecture, serve to give it consequence, and add to the gaiety, splendor, and bustle of the scenery.

Round the main habitation, and near all their decorated structures, the grounds are laid out with great regularity, and kept with great care: no plants are admitted that intercept the view of the buildings; nor no lines but such as accompany the architecture properly, and contribute to the general good effect of the whole composition: for they hold it absurd to surround an elegant fabric with disorderly rude vegetation; saying, that it looks like a diamond set in lead; and always conveys the idea of an unfinished work. When the buildings are rustic, the scenery which surrounds them is wild; when they are grand, it is gloomy; when gay, it is luxuriant: in short, the Chinese are scrupulously nice in preserving

the

the fame character through every part of the compofition; which is one great caufe of that furprizing variety with which their works abound.

They are fond of introducing ftatues, bufts, bas-reliefs, and every production of the chifel, as well in other parts of their Gardens, as round their buildings; obferving, that they are not only ornamental, but that by commemorating paft events, and celebrated perfonages, they awaken the mind to pleafing contemplation, hurrying our reflections up into the remoteft ages of antiquity: and they never fail to fcatter antient infcriptions, verfes, and moral fentences, about their grounds; which are placed on large ruinated ftones, and columns of marble, or engraved on trees and rocks; fuch fituations being always chofen for them, as correfpond with the fenfe of the infcriptions; which thereby acquire additional force in themfelves, and likewife give a ftronger expreffion to the fcene.

They fay that all thefe decorations are neceffary, to characterize and diftinguifh the different fcenes of their compositions; among which, without such assistance, there must unavoidably be a tiresome similarity.

And whenever it is objected to them, that many of these things are unnatural, and ought therefore not to be suffered, they say, that most improvements are unnatural, yet they are allowed to be improvements, and not only tolerated, but admired. Our vestments, say they, are neither of leather, nor like our skins, but formed of rich silks and embroidery; our houses and palaces bear no resemblance to caverns in the rocks, which are the only natural habitations; nor is our music either like thunder, or the whistling of the northern wind, the harmony of nature. Nature produces nothing either boiled, roasted or stewed, and yet we do not eat raw meat; nor doth she supply us with any other tools for all our purposes, but teeth and hands; yet we have saws, hammers, axes, and a thousand other implements: in short, there is scarcely any thing in which art is not apparent; and why should its appearance be excluded from Gardening only? Poets and painters soar above the pitch of nature, when they

they would give energy to their compofitions. The fame privilege, therefore, fhould be allowed to Gardeners: inanimate, fimple nature, is too infipid for our purpofes; much is expected from us; and therefore, we have occafion for every aid that either art or nature can furnifh. The fcenery of a garden fhould differ as much from common nature as an heroic poem doth from a profe relation; and Gardeners, like poets, fhould give a loofe to their imagination, and even fly beyond the bounds of truth, whenever it is neceffary to elevate, to embellifh, to enliven, or to add novelty to their fubject.

The ufual method of diftributing Gardens in China, is to contrive a great variety of fcenes, to be feen from certain points of view; at which are placed feats or buildings, adapted to the different purpofes of mental or fenfual enjoyments. The perfection of their Gardens confifts in the number and diverfity of thefe fcenes; and in the artful combination of their parts; which they endeavour to difpofe in fuch a manner, as not only feparately to appear to the beft advantage, but alfo to unite in forming an elegant and ftriking whole.

Where the ground is extenſive, and many ſcenes can be introduced, they generally adapt each to one ſingle point of view; but where it is confined, and affords no room for variety, they diſpoſe their objects ſo, that being viewed from different points, they produce different repreſentations; and often ſuch as bear no reſemblance to each other. They likewiſe endeavour to place the ſeparate ſcenes of their compoſitions in ſuch directions as to unite, and be ſeen all together, from one or more particular points of view, whence the eye may be delighted with an extenſive, rich and variegated proſpect. They take all poſſible advantage of exterior objects; hiding carefully the boundaries of their own grounds; and endeavouring to make an apparent union between them and the diſtant woods, fields and rivers: and where towns, caſtles, towers, or any other conſiderable objects are in ſight, they artfully contrive to have them ſeen from as many points, and in as many directions as poſſible. The ſame they do with regard to navigable rivers, high roads, foot-paths, mills, and all other moving objects, which animate and add variety to the landſcape.

Beſides

Besides the usual European methods of concealing boundaries by ha-has, and sunk fences, they have others, still more effectual. On flats, where they have naturally no prospects of exterior objects, they enclose their plantations with artificial terrasses, in the form of walks, to which you ascend by insensible slopes: these they border on the inside with thickets of lofty trees and underwood; and on the outside, with low shrubberies; over which the passenger sees the whole scenery of the adjacent country, in appearance forming a continuation of the Garden, as its fence is carefully concealed amongst the shrubs that cover the outside declivity of the terrass.

And where the Garden happens to stand on higher ground than the adjacent country, they carry artificial rivers round the outskirts, under the opposite banks of which the boundaries are concealed, amongst trees and shrubs. Sometimes too they make use of strong wire fences, painted green, fastened to the trees and shrubs that border the plantations, and carried round in many irregular directions, which are scarcely seen till you come very near them: and wherever ha-has, or funk fences are ufed, they always fill the trenches with briars, and other thorny plants, to ftrengthen the fence, and to conceal the walls, which otherwife would have an ugly appearance from without.

In their large Gardens they contrive different fcenes for the different times of the day; difpofing at the points of view buildings, which from their ufe point out the proper hour for enjoying the view in its perfections. And in their fmall ones, where, as has been obferved, one arrangement produces many reprefentations, they make ufe of the fame artifice. They have befide, fcenes for every feafon of the year: fome for winter, generally expofed to the fouthern fun, and compofed of pines, firs, cedars, evergreen oaks, phillyreas, hollies, yews, and many other evergreens; being enriched with laurels of various forts, laureftinus, arbutus, and other plants and vegetables that grow and flourifh in cold weather: and to give variety and gaiety to thefe gloomy productions, they plant amongft them, in regular forms, divided by

walks,

walks, all the rare shrubs, flowers and trees of the torrid zone; which they cover, during the winter, with frames of glass, disposed in the forms of temples, and other elegant buildings. These they call conservatiories; they are warmed by subterraneous fires, and afford a comfortable and agreeable retreat, when the weather is too cold to walk in the open air. All sorts of beautiful and melodious birds are let loose in them: and they keep there, in large porcelain cisterns, placed on artificial rocks, gold and silver fishes; with various kinds of aquatic plants and flowers: they also raise in them strawberries, cherries, figs, grapes, apricots and peaches, which cover the wood-work of their glass frames, and serve for ornament as well as use.

Their scenes of spring likewise abound with evergreens, intermixed with lilacks of all sorts, laburnums, limes, larixes, double blossomed thorn, almond and peach-trees; with sweet-bryar, early roses, and honey-suckles. The ground, and verges of the thickets and shrubberies, are adorned with wild hyacinths, wall-flowers, daffodils, violets,

violets, primroses, polianthes's, crocus's, daisies, snowdrops, and various species of the iris; with such other flowers as appear in the months of March and April: and as these scenes are also scanty in their natural productions, they intersperse amongst their plantations, menageries for all sorts of tame and ferocious animals, and birds of prey; aviaries and groves, with proper contrivances for breeding domestic fowls; decorated dairies; and buildings for the exercises of wrestling, boxing, quail-fighting, and other games known in China. They also contrive in the woods large open recesses for military sports; as riding, vaulting, fencing, shooting with the bow, and running.

Their summer scenes compose the richest and most studied parts of their Gardens. They abound with lakes, rivers, and water-works of every contrivance; and with vessels of every construction, calculated for the uses of sailing, rowing, fishing, fowling, and fighting. The woods consist of oak, beech, Indian chesnut, elm, ash, plane, sycamore, maple, abele and several other species of

the

the poplar; with many other trees, peculiar to China. The thickets are compofed of every fair deciduous plant that grows in that climate, and every flower or fhrub that flourifhes during the fummer months; all uniting to form the fineft verdure, the moft brilliant, harmonious colouring imaginable. The buildings are fpacious, fplendid and numerous; every fcene being marked by one or more: fome of them contrived for banquets, balls, concerts, learned difputations, plays, rope-dancing, and feats of activity; others again for bathing, fwimming, reading, fleeping, or meditation.

In the center of thefe fummer plantations, there is generally a large tract of ground fet afide for more fecret and voluptuous enjoyments; which is laid out in a great number of clofe walks, colonades and paffages, turned with many intricate windings, fo as to confufe and lead the paffenger aftray; being fometimes divided by thickets of underwood, intermixed with ftraggling large trees; and at other times by higher plantations, or by clumps of rofe-trees, and other lofty flowering fhrubs. The whole

whole is a wildernefs of fweets, adorned with all forts of fragrant and gaudy productions: gold and filver pheafants, pea-fowls, partridges, bantam hens, quails, and game of every kind, fwarm in the woods; doves, nightingales, and a thoufand melodious birds, perch upon the branches; deer, antelopes, fpotted buffaloes, fheep, and Tartarean horfes, frifk upon the plains: every walk leads to fome delightful object; to groves of orange and myrtle; to rivulets, whofe banks are clad with rofes, woodbine and jeffamine; to murmuring fountains, with ftatues of fleeping nymphs, and water-gods; to cabinets of verdure, with beds of aromatic herbs and flowers; to grottos cut in rocks, adorned with incruftations of coral fhells, ores, gems and chriftalifations, refrefhed with rills of fweet fcented water, and cooled by fragrant, artificial breezes.

Amongft the thickets which divide the walks, are many fecret receffes; in each of which there is an elegant pavilion, confifting of one ftate-apartment, with outhoufes, and proper conveniences for eunuchs and women-fervants.

fervants. Thefe are inhabited, during the fummer, by their faireft and moft accomplifhed concubines; each of them, with her attendants, occupying a feparate pavilion.

The principal apartment of thefe buildings, confifts of one or more large faloons, two cabinet or dreffing-rooms, a library, a couple of bed-chambers and waiting-rooms, a bath, and feveral private clofets; all which are magnificently furnifhed, and provided with entertaining books, amorous paintings, mufical inftruments, implements for gaming, writing, drawing, painting and embroidering; with beds, couches, and chairs, of various conftructions, for the ufes of fitting and lying in different poftures.

The faloons generally open to little enclofed courts, fet round with beautiful flower-pots, of different forms, made of porcelain, marble or copper, filled with the rareft flowers of the feafon: at the end of the court there is generally an aviary; an artificial rock with a fountain

and

and bason for gold fish; a cascade; an arbor of bamboo or vine interwoven with flowering shrubs; or some other elegant contrivance, of the like nature.

Besides these separate habitations, in which the ladies are privately visited by the patron, as often as he is disposed to see them, there are, in other larger recesses of the thickets, more splendid and spacious buildings, where the women all meet at certain hours of the day, either to eat at the public tables, to drink their tea, to converse, bathe, swim, work, romp, or to play at the mora, and other games known in China; or else to divert the patron with music, singing, lascivious posture-dancing, and acting plays or pantomines; at all which they generally are very expert.

Some of these structures are entirely open; the roof being supported on columns of rose-wood, or cedar, with bases of Corean jasper; or upon wooden pillars, made in imitation of bamboo, and plantane-trees, surrounded with garlands of fruit and flowers, artfully carved, being

painted

painted and varnished in proper colours. Others are enclosed; and consist sometimes only of one spacious hall, and sometimes of many different sized rooms, of various forms; as triangles, squares, hexagons, octagons, circles, ovals, and irregular whimsical shapes; all of them elegantly finished with incrustations of marble, inlaid precious woods, ivory, silver, gold, and mother of pearl; with a profusion of antient porcelain, mirrors, carving, gilding, painting and lacquering of all colours.

The doors of entrance to these apartments, are circular and polygonal, as well as rectangular: and the windows by which they are lighted, are made in the shapes of fans, birds, animals, fishes, insects, leaves and flowers; being filled with painted glass, or different coloured gauſe, to tinge the light, and give a glow to the objects in the apartment.

All these buildings are furnished at a very great expence, not only with the necessary moveables, but with pictures, sculptures, embroideries, trinkets, and pieces of clock-work of great value, being some of them very large, composed of many ingenious movements, and enriched with ornaments of gold, intermixed with pearls, diamonds, rubies, emeralds, and other gems.

Besides the different structures already mentioned, they have some made in the form of Persian tents; others built of roots and pollards, put together with great taste; and others, called Miau Ting, or Halls of the Moon, of a prodigious size; composed each of one single vaulted room, made in the shape of a hemisphere; the concave of which is artfully painted, in imitation of a nocturnal sky, and pierced with an infinite number of little windows, made to represent the moon and stars, being filled with tinged glass, that admits the light in the quantities necessary to spread over the whole interior fabric the pleasing gloom of a fine summer's night.

The pavements of these rooms are sometimes laid out in parterres of flowers; amongst which are placed many rural seats, made of fine formed branches, varnished red

to

to reprefent coral: but oftenest their bottom is full of a clear running water, which falls in rills from the fides of a rock in the center; many little iflands float upon its furface, and move around as the current directs; fome of them covered with tables for the banquet; others with feats for muficians; and others with arbors, containing beds of repofe, with fophas, feats, and other furniture, for various ufes.

To thefe halls of the moon the Chinefe princes retire, with their favourite women, whenever the heat and intenfe light of the fummer's day becomes difagreeable to them; and here they feaft, and give a loofe to every fort of voluptuous pleafure.

No nation ever equalled the Chinefe in the fplendor and number of their garden ftructures. We are told by Father Attiret, that in one of the imperial gardens near Pekin, called Yven Ming Yven, there are, befides the palace, which is of itfelf a city, four hundred pavilions, all fo different in their architecture, that

each

each seems the production of a different country. He mentions one of them, that cost upwards of two hundred thousand pounds, exclusive of the furniture; another, consisting of a hundred rooms: and says, that most of them are sufficiently capacious to lodge the greatest European lord, and his whole retinue. There is likewise, in the same garden, a fortified town, with its port, streets, public squares, temples, markets, shops, and tribunals of justice: in short, with every thing that is at Pekin; only upon a smaller scale.

In this town the emperors of China, who are too much the slaves of their greatness to appear in public, and their women, who are excluded from it by custom, are frequently diverted with the hurry and bustle of the capital; which is there represented, several times in the year, by the eunuchs of the palace: some of them personating merchants, others artists, artificers, officers, soldiers, shopkeepers, porters, and even thieves and pickpockets. On the appointed day, each puts on the habit of his profession: the ships arrive at the port, the shops are opened,

and

and the goods are offered to fale; tea-houfes, taverns, and inns, are ready for the reception of company; fruits, and all forts of refrefhments, are cried about the ftreets: the fhop-keepers teize the paffengers to purchafe their merchandize; and every liberty is permitted: there is no diftinction of perfons; even the emperor is confounded in the crowd: quarrels happen---battles enfue---the watch feizes upon the combatants---they are conveyed before the judge, he examines the difpute and condemns the culprit, who is fometimes very feverely baftinadoed, to divert his imperial majefty, and the ladies of his train.

Neither are fharpers forgot in thefe feftivals; that noble profeffion is generally allotted to a good number of the moft dextrous eunuchs, who, like the Spartan youths of old, are punifhed or applauded, according to the merit of their exploits.

The plantations of their autumnal fcenes confift of many forts of oak, beech, and other deciduous trees that are retentive of the leaf, and afford in their decline a

rich

rich variegated colouring; with which they blend some ever-greens, some fruit-trees, and the few shrubs and flowers which blossom late in the year; placing amongst them decayed trees, pollards, and dead stumps, of picturesque forms, overspread with moss and ivy.

The buildings with which these scenes are decorated, are generally such as indicate decay, being intended as mementos to the passenger. Some are hermitages and alms-houses, where the faithful old servants of the family spend the remains of life in peace, amidst the tombs of their predecessors, who lie buried around them: others are ruins of castles, palaces, temples, and deserted religious houses; or half buried triumphal arches and mausoleums, with mutilated inscriptions, that once commemorated the heroes of antient times; or they are sepulchres of their ancestors, catacombs and cemeteries for their favourite domestic animals; or whatever else may serve to indicate the debility, the disappointments, and the dissolution of humanity; which, by co-operating with the dreary aspect of autumnal nature, and the inclement tem-
perature

perature of the air, fill the mind with melancholy, and incline it to ferious reflections.

Such is the common fcenery of the Chinefe Gardens, where the ground has no ftriking tendency to any particular character. But where it is more ftrongly marked, their artifts never fail to improve upon its fingularities; their aim is to excite a great variety of paffions in the mind of the fpectator; and the fertility of their imaginations, always upon the ftretch in fearch of novelty, furnifhes them with a thoufand artifices to accomplifh that aim.

The fcenes which I have hitherto defcribed, are chiefly of the pleafing kind: but the Chinefe Gardeners have many forts, which they employ as circumftances vary; all which they range in three feparate claffes; and diftinguifh them by the appellations of the pleafing, the terrible, and the furprizing.

The firft of thefe are compofed of the gayeft and moft perfect productions of the vegetable world; intermixed
with.

with rivers, lakes, cafcades, fountains, and water-works of all forts: being combined and difpofed in all the picturefque forms that art or nature can fuggeft. Buildings, fculptures, and paintings are added, to give fplendor and variety to thefe compofitions; and the rareft productions of the animal creation are collected, to enliven them: nothing is forgot that can either exhilerate the mind, gratify the fenfes, or give a fpur to the imagination.

Their fcenes of terror are compofed of gloomy woods, deep vallies inacceffible to the fun, impending barren rocks, dark caverns, and impetuous cataracts rufhing down the mountains from all parts. The trees are ill formed, forced out of their natural directions, and feemingly torn to pieces by the violence of tempefts: fome are thrown down, and intercept the courfe of the torrents; others look as if blafted and fhattered by the power of lightening: the buildings are in ruins; or half confumed by fire, or fwept away by the fury of the waters: nothing remaining entire but a few miferable huts difperfed in the mountains, which ferve at once to indicate

the

the exiftence and wretchednefs of the inhabitants. Bats, owls, vultures, and every bird of prey flutter in the groves; wolves, tigers and jackalls howl in the forefts; half-famifhed animals wander upon the plains; gibbets, croffes, wheels, and the whole apparatus of torture, are feen from the roads; and in the moft difmal receffes of the woods, where the ways are rugged and overgrown with weeds, and where every object bears the marks of depopulation, are temples dedicated to the king of vengeance, deep caverns in the rocks, and defcents to fubterraneous habitations, overgrown with brufhwood and brambles; near which are placed pillars of ftone, with pathetic defcriptions of tragical events, and many horrid acts of cruelty, perpetrated there by outlaws and robbers of former times: and to add both to the horror and fublimity of thefe fcenes, they fometimes conceal in cavities, on the fummits of the higheft mountains, founderies, lime-kilns, and glafs-works; which fend forth large volumes of flame, and continued columns of thick fmoke, that give to thefe mountains the appearance of volcanoes.

Their surprizing, or supernatural scenes, are of the romantic kind, and abound in the marvellous; being calculated to excite in the minds of the spectators, quick successions of opposite and violent sensations. Sometimes the passenger is hurried by steep descending paths to subterraneous vaults, divided into apartments, where lamps, which yield a faint glimmering light, discover the pale images of antient kings and heroes, reclining on beds of state; their heads are crowned with garlands of stars, and in their hands are tablets of moral sentences: flutes, and soft harmonious organs, impelled by subterraneous waters, interrupt, at stated intervals, the silence of the place, and fill the air with solemn melody.

Sometimes the traveller, after having wandered in the dusk of the forest, finds himself on the edge of precipices, in the glare of day-light, with cataracts falling from the mountains around, and torrents raging in the depths beneath him; or at the foot of impending rocks, in gloomy vallies, overhung with woods, on the banks of dull moving rivers, whose shores are covered with sepulchral monuments,

monuments, under the shade of willows, laurels, and other plants, sacred to Manchew, the genius of sorrow.

His way now lies through dark passages cut in the rocks, on the side of which are recesses, filled with colossal figures of dragons, infernal fiends, and other horrid forms, which hold in their monstrous talons, mysterious, cabalistical sentences, inscribed on tables of brass; with preparations that yield a constant flame; serving at once to guide and to astonish the passenger: from time to time he is surprized with repeated shocks of electrical impulse, with showers of artificial rain, or sudden violent gusts of wind, and instantaneous explosions of fire; the earth trembles under him, by the power of confined air; and his ears are successively struck with many different sounds, produced by the same means; some resembling the cries of men in torment; others the roaring of bulls, and howl of ferocious animals, with the yell of hounds, and the voices of hunters; others are like the mixed croaking of ravenous birds; and others imitate thunder, the raging of the

sea,

sea, the explosion of cannon, the sound of trumpets, and all the noise of war.

His road then lies through lofty woods, where serpents and lizards of many beautiful sorts crawl upon the ground, and where innumerable monkies, cats and parrots, clamber upon the trees, and intimidate him as he passes; or through flowery thickets, where he is delighted with the singing of birds, the harmony of flutes, and all kinds of soft instrumental music: sometimes, in this romantic excursion, the passenger finds himself in extensive recesses, surrounded with arbors of jessamine, vine and roses, where beauteous Tartarean damsels, in loose transparent robes, that flutter in the air, present him with rich wines, mangostans, ananas, and fruits of Quangsi; crown him with garlands of flowers, and invite him to taste the sweets of retirement, on Persian carpets, and beds of camusath skin down.

These enchanted scenes always abound with water-works, so contrived as to produce many surprizing effects; and

and many splendid pieces of scenery. Air is likewise employed with great success, on different occasions; not only for the purposes above-mentioned, but likewise to form artificial and complicated echoes: some repeating the motion of the feet; some the rustling of garments; and others the human voice, in many different tones: all which are calculated to embarrass, to surprize, or to terrify the passenger in his progress.

All sorts of optical deceptions are also made use of; such as paintings on prepared surfaces, contrived to vary the representations as often as the spectator changes place: exhibiting, in one view, groupes of men; in another, combats of animals; in a third, rocks, cascades, trees and mountains; in a fourth, temples and colonades; and a variety of other pleasing subjects. They likewise contrive pavements and incrustations for the walls of their apartments, of Mosaic work, composed of many pieces of marble, seemingly thrown together without order or design; which, when seen from certain points of view, unite in forming lively and exact representations of men,

animals,

animals, buildings and landscapes: and they frequently introduce pieces of architecture, and even whole prospects in perspective; which are formed by introducing temples, bridges, vessels, and other fixed objects, lessened as they are more distant from the points of view, by giving greyish tints to the distant parts of the composition; and by planting there trees of a fainter colour, and smaller growth, than those that appear in the fore ground: thus rendering considerable in appearance, what in reality is trifling.

The Chinese Artists introduce into these enchanted scenes, all kinds of sensitive, and other extraordinary trees, plants and flowers. They keep in them a surprizing variety of monstrous birds, reptiles, and animals, which they import from distant countries, or obtain by crossing the breeds. These are tamed by art; and guarded by enormous dogs of Tibet, and African giants, in the habits of magicians.

They likewise have amongst the plantations, cabinets,
in

in which are collected all the extraordinary productions of the animal, vegetable and mineral kingdoms; as well as paintings, sculptures, medals, antiquities, and ingenious inventions of the mechanic arts: which are a fresh source of entertainment, when the weather is bad, or when the heat is too intense to admit of being in the open air.

The communications to the different scenes and other parts of the Chinese Gardens, are by walks, roads, bridle-ways, navigable rivers, lakes, and canals; in all which their artists introduce as much variety as possible; not only in the forms and dimensions, but also in their decoration: avoiding, nevertheless, all the absurdities with which our antient European style of Gardening abounds.

" I am not ignorant," said one of their artists, " that
" your European planters, thinking Nature scanty in her
" arrangements, or being perhaps disgusted with the fa-
" miliarity and commonness of natural objects, introduce
" artificial forms into their plantations, and cut their
" trees in the shapes of pyramids, flower-pots, men,
" fishes,

" fishes, and brute animals; and I have heard of colo-
" nades, and whole palaces, formed by plants, cut as
" precisely as if they had been built of stone. But this is
" purchasing variety at the expence of reason: such ex-
" travagancies ought never to be tolerated, excepting in
" enchanted scenes: and there but very seldom; for they
" must be as destitute of beauty, as they are of propriety;
" and if the planter be a traveller, and a man of ob-
" servation, he can want no such helps to variety, as he
" will recollect a thousand beautiful effects along the
" common roads of the countries through which he has
" passed, that may be introduced with much better
" success."

Their roads, walks and avenues, are either directed in a single straight line, twisted in a crooked one, or carried zig-zag, by several straight lines, altering their course at certain points. They observe that there are few objects more strikingly great than a spacious road, planted on each side with lofty trees, and stretching in a direct line, beyond the reach of the eye; and that there are few things

more

more varioufly entertaining, than a winding one, which opening gradually to the fight, difcovers, at every ftep, a new arrangement; and although, in itfelf, it has not the power of raifing violent emotions, yet, by bringing the paffenger fuddenly and unexpectedly to great or uncommon things, it occafions ftrong impreffions of furprize and aftonifhment, which are more forcibly felt, as being more oppofite to the tranquil pleafure enjoyed in the confined parts of the road: and, in fmall compofitions, they find crooked directions exceedingly ufeful to the planter, who, by winding his walks, may give an idea of great extent, notwithftanding the narrownefs of his limits.

They fay that roads which are compofed of repeated ftraight lines, altering their directions at certain points, have all the advantages both of crooked and ftraight ones, with other properties, peculiar to themfelves. The variety and new arrangement of objects, fay they, which prefent themfelves at every change of direction, occupy the mind agreeably: their abrupt appearance occafions furprize;

M. which,

which, when the extent is vaft, and the repetitions frequent, fwells into aftonifhment and admiration: the incertitude of the mind where thefe repetitions will end, and its anxiety as the fpectator approaches towards the periods, are likewife very ftrong impreffions, preventing that ftate of languor into which the mind naturally finks by dwelling long on the fame objects.

The ftraight directions, particularly the zig-zag, are, on account of thefe effects, well adapted to avenues or high roads, which lead to towns, palaces, bridges, or triumphal arches; to caftles or prifons, for the reception of criminals; to maufoleums; and all other works of which the intent is to infpire horror, veneration or aftonifhment. To humbler objects, the waving line is a more proper approach; the fmallnefs of their parts rendering them unfit for a diftant infpection: and as they are trifling in themfelves, they pleafe moft when their appearance is unexpected: and from the very point whence all their little beauties are feen in the higheft luftre.

In difposing the walks of their Gardens, the Chinese artists are very attentive to lead them succeffively to all the principal buildings, fine profpects, and other interefting parts of the compofition; that the paffenger may be conducted infenfibly, as it were by accident, and without turning back, or feeming to go out of the way, to every object deferving notice.

Both their ftraight and winding walks are, in fome places, kept at a confiderable diftance from each other, and feparated by clofe planted thickets, to hide all exterior objects; as well to keep the paffenger in fufpenfe with regard to the extent, as to excite thofe gloomy fenfations which naturally fteal upon the mind, in wandering through the intricacies of a folitary foreft. In other places the walks approach each other; and the thickets growing gradually lefs deep, and more thinly planted, the ear is ftruck with the voices of thofe who are in the adjacent walks, and the eye amufed with a confufed fight of their perfons, between the ftems and foliage of the trees. Infenfibly again the plantations fpread and darken,

darken, the objects disappear, and the voices die in confused murmurs; when unexpectedly the walks are turned into the same open spaces, and the different companies are agreeably surprized to meet where they may view each other, and satisfy their curiosity without impediment.

The Chinese Gardeners very seldom finish any of their walks *en cul de sac*; carefully avoiding all unpleasant disappointments: but if at any time the nature of the situation obliges them to it, they always terminate at some interesting object; which lessens the disappointment, and takes off the idea of a childish conceit.

Neither do they ever carry a walk round the extremities of a piece of ground, and leave the middle entirely open, as it is too often done amongst us: for though it might render the first glance striking and noble, they think the pleasure would be of short duration; and that the spectator would be but moderately entertained, by walking several miles, with the same objects continually
obtruding

obtruding upon his fight. If the ground they have to work upon be fmall, and that they choofe to exhibit a grand fcene, either from the principal habitation, or any other capital point, they do indeed leave a great part of the fpace open; but ftill care is taken to have a good depth of thicket, which frequently breaks confiderably in upon the open fpace, and hides many parts of it from the fpectator's eye.

Thefe projections produce variety, by altering the apparent figure of the open fpace from every point of view; and by conftantly hiding parts of it, they create a myftery which excites the traveller's curiofity: they likewife occafion, in many places, a great depth in the thicket, to make receffes for buildings, feats, and other objects, as well as for bold windings of the principal walks, and for feveral fmaller paths to branch off from the principal ones; all which take off the idea of a boundary, and afford amufement to the paffenger in his courfe: and as it is not eafy to purfue all the turns of the different lateral paths, there is ftill fomething left

left to defire, and a field for the imagination to work upon.

In their crooked walks, they carefully avoid all fudden or unnatural windings, particularly the regular ferpentine curves, of which our Englifh Gardeners are fo fond; obferving, that thefe eternal, uniform, undulating lines, are, of all things, the moft unnatural, the moft affected, and moft tirefome to purfue. Having nature in view, they feldom turn their walks, without fome apparent excufe; either to avoid impediments, naturally exifting, or raifed by art, to improve the fcenery. A mountain, a precipice, a deep valley, a marfh, a piece of rugged ground, a building, or fome old venerable plant, afford a ftriking reafon for turning afide; and if a river, the fea, a wide extended lake, or a terrace commanding rich profpects, prefent themfelves, they hold it judicious to follow them in all their windings; fo to protract the enjoyments which thefe noble objects procure: but on a plain, either open, or formed into groves and thickets, where no impediments oblige, nor no curiofity invites to follow

follow a winding path, they think it abfurd, faying, that the road muft either have been made by art, or be worn by the conftant paffage of travellers; in either of which cafes, it cannot be fuppofed that men would go by a crooked line, where they could arrive by a ftraight one. In general, they are very fparing of their twifts, which are always eafy, and fo managed that never more than one curve is perceptible at the fame time.

They likewife take care to avoid an exact parallelifm in thefe walks, both with regard to the trees which border them, and the ground of which they are compofed. The ufual width given to the walk, is from eight to twenty, or even thirty feet, according to the extent of the plantation; but the trees, on each fide, are, in many places, more diftant; large fpaces being left open, and covered with grafs and wild flowers, or with fern, broom, briars, and underwood.

The ground of the walk is either of turf or gravel; neither of them finifhing exactly at its edges, but running

ning some way into the thickets, groves or shrubberies, on each side; in order to imitate nature more closely, and to take off that disagreeable formality and stiffness, which a contrary practice occasions in our European plantations.

In their straight roads or walks, when the extent is vast, the Chinese artists observe an exact order and symmetry, saying, that in stupendous works, the appearance of art is by no means disgusting; that it conveys to posterity instances of the grandeur of their ancestors; and gives birth to many sublime and pleasing reflections. The imperial roads are astonishing works of this nature; they are composed of triple avenues, adorned with four rows of enormous trees; generally Indian chesnuts, spruce firs, mountain cedars, and others of formal shapes; or oaks, elms, tulips, and others of the largest growth, planted at proper regular distances; and extending in straight lines, and almost on a perfect level, two, three, even four hundred miles. The center avenues are from one hundred and fifty, to two hundred feet wide; and the lateral ones,

ones, are generally from forty to fifty feet; the spreading branches of the trees forming over them a natural umbrella, under which the travellers pass, at all times of the day, unmolested by the sun.

In some places these roads are carried, by lofty vaulted passages, through the rocks and mountains; in others, upon causeways and bridges, over lakes, torrents, and arms of the sea; and in others, they are supported, between the precipices, upon chains of iron, or upon pillars, and many tire of arcades, over villages, pagodas, and cities: in short, no difficulty has been attended to in their construction; but every obstacle has been conquered with amazing industry, and at an almost incredible expence.

There are, in different parts of China, many works of the kinds just mentioned; but amongst the most considerable, are counted the Passage of King-tong, the Bridges of Fo-cheu and Lo-yang, and the Cientao, in the province of Xensi.

The firft of thefe is a communication between two precipices, compofed of twenty enormous chains of iron, each two hundred feet in length, which are covered with planks and earth, to form the road.

The fecond is a bridge between Fo-cheu and the fuburb Nan-ti, confifting of one hundred arches, of a fufficient fize for the paffage of fhips under full fail: it is built of large blocks of hewn ftone, and enclofed with a magnificent marble baluftrade, the pedeftals of which fupport two hundred coloffal lions, artfully cut in the fame material.

The bridge of Lo-yang is in the province of Fokien, and is the largeft and moft furprizing work of the fort that yet has been heard of. It is compofed of three hundred piers of black marble, joined to each other by vaft blocks of the fame material, forming the road, which is enclofed with a marble baluftrade, whofe pedeftals are adorned with lions, and other works of fculpture. The whole length of the bridge is fixteen thoufand two hundred feet,

feet, or upwards of three miles; its width is forty-two feet; and the blocks of which it is compofed are each fifty-four feet long, and fix feet diameter.

The Cientao, or Way of Pillars, is a communication between many precipices, built to fhorten the road to Pekin. It is near four miles long, of a confiderable width, and fupported over the vallies upon arches and ftone piers of a terrifying height.

In the mountains, on each fide of thefe imperial roads, are erected a great number of buildings, adorned with coloffal ftatues, and other works of fculpture, which afford conftant entertainment to the paffengers. Thefe are the monuments of their wife men, their faints, and their warriors, erected at the expence of the ftate, and furnifhed with nervous infcriptions, in the Chinefe language, giving an account of the lives and actions of thofe they commemorate: fome of thefe buildings are diftributed into many fpacious courts and ftately apartments, being little inferior to palaces, either in magnificence or extent.

Inftead

Instead of roads, the center avenues are sometimes formed into navigable canals, from one hundred to one hundred and fifty feet wide, being sufficiently deep to admit galleys and other small vessels; with horse-ways on each side of the canals, for the convenience of towing them, either against the wind or the stream. On these the emperor, and Chinese mandarines, are frequently conveyed, in large magnificent sampans or barges, divided into many splendid rooms; being sometimes attended by a considerable train of smaller vessels, of different constructions, adorned with dragons, streamers, lanterns of painted silk, and various other ornaments, the whole composing a very brilliant and entertaining show.

All the imperial forests, besides the high roads which pass through them, have many spacious avenues cut in the woods, spreading from different centers, like rays of stars, and terminating at idol temples, towers, castles, and all the interesting objects of the circumjacent country. The centers from which these avenues part, are of a circular or octagonal figure, with eight avenues; or of a semi-
circular

circular form, with only three branching from them. Their area is generally very confiderable; and its middle is adorned with a triumphal arch, a pagoda, a magnificent fountain, or fome other confiderable monument.

Where the extent is vaft, each fingle avenue has befides, in its courfe, one or more open fpaces, from which a number of fmaller avenues again branch out, and terminate at many buildings, erected in the woods, for various purpofes; all which, without any confufion, add to the variety and intricacy of thefe compofitions; giving them an appearance of immenfity not to be conceived, but by fuch as have feen them: and wherever a deep valley, a large river, or an arm of the fea, interrupt and break off the courfe of the avenues, the plantations are neverthelefs continued on the oppofite fhore, in order to make them appear more confiderable.

In ftraight roads, of fmaller dimenfions, the Chinefe very artfully imitate the irregular workings of nature; for although the general direction be a ftraight line, yet they
eafily

eafily avoid all appearance of ftiffnefs or formality, by planting fome of the trees out of the common line; by inclining fome of them out of an upright; or by employing different fpecies of plants, and by placing them at irregular diftances, with their ftems fometimes bare, and at other times covered with honey-fuckles and fweetbryar, or furrounded with underwood. They likewife cut and difpofe the branches of the trees in various manners; fome being fuffered to fpread, to cover and fhade the walks; whilft others are fhortened, to admit the fun. The ground too is compofed of rifes and falls; and the banks on each fide of the walk are, in fome places, of a confiderable height, forming hollow ways, which they often cover at the top with bufhes and trunks of fallen trees: frequently too the courfe of the walk is interrupted by a large oak, or elm, or tulipifera, placed in the middle; or by a fcreen of trees running quite acrofs; which, when the part on one fide of the fcreen is opened and iluminated by the fun, and the part on the other fide, clofe and fhaded, produces a pleafing contraft.

I have

I have often seen, in China, *berceaus* and arbors, not of lattice-work, as in France, but of bamboo, hazel, and elm, whose branches being interwoven at the top, formed an arch not at all displeasing to the eye, and exceedingly useful, during the heats of summer: and to render these cool retreats more agreeable, jessamine, scarlet beans, sweet-scented pease, granadillas of several sorts, nasturtiums, the convulvus major, and many other sorts of climbers, were planted round the outside, which, forcing their way through, enriched the sides and arches of the walks in a very beautiful manner.

I have likewise seen, in Chinese plantations, walks bordered with the cut yew and elm hedges, so common in most countries of Europe, which the Chinese artists sometimes admit of, for variety's sake; but they never have the stiff appearance of our European ones: the shears are used sparingly; towards the top the branches are suffered to spread unmolested; and even in the cut parts of them are seen large masses of other plants forcing their way through; such as the sycamore, the fig, the vine, and

and others, whose foliage and verdure are most opposite to those of the hedge.

The dimensions both of their straight roads and walks, vary according to the purposes they are designed for; and, in some degree too, according to their length. Roads or avenues to considerable objects, are, as has been observed, generally composed of three parallel walks: that in the middle being from thirty to one hundred and fifty, or even two hundred feet wide; those on the sides, from fifteen to forty. In their Gardens, the principal straight walks are never narrower than twenty feet; and seldom broader than forty-five or fifty: and the smallest straight walks are at least twelve feet wide. Thirty to thirty-six feet is called a sufficient width for a length of two hundred yards; forty to fifty for one of four hundred; sixty for one of six hundred; and seventy for a length of eight hundred yards: and when the extent is more than this last dimension, they do not tie themselves up to any proportion, but encrease their width as much as they conveniently can; never, however, exceeding one hundred and

and fifty, to two hundred feet; which they think the utmost width that can be given, without rendering the avenue disproportionate to the trees that border it.

In the construction of roads and walks, the Chinese Gardeners are very expert, and very circumspect: they never situate them at the foot of mountains or rising grounds, without contriving drains to receive the waters descending from the heights, which are afterwards discharged by arched gulleys under the roads, into the plains below; forming, in the rainy season, a great number of little cascades, that increase the beauty of the scenery. The roads which are designed for carriages, they make as level as possible; they give them a solid bottom, and shape them so as to throw off the rain-waters expeditiously: they use, as much as possible, the nearest materials, to save expence; and are very judicious in employing different soils to form mixtures, which never become either hard or slippery; never loose in dry weather, nor deep in wet; not easily ground into powder; nor ever forming a rough flinty surface, difficult and painful for horses to move upon.

Their walks are either of grafs, of gravel, or chippings of ftone, covered with a fmall quantity of coarfe river-fand. The firft fort, which are feldom ufed but in private Gardens, they being too liable to be fpoiled in public walks, are made of the fineft and cleaneft turf that can be found on downs and commons; and they are kept in order, by frequent mowing, and rowling with large iron rowlers. The fecond fort are made of binding gravel, laid about fix inches deep, upon the natural ground: if it be dry, or if fwampy, upon brick rubbifh, flint ftones, or any other hard materials, eafieft to be had: and thefe are alfo kept firm, and in great beauty, by frequent rowling. Thofe of ftone are compofed of gallets, laid about a foot thick, rammed to a firm confiftence, and a regular furface; upon which is laid a fufficient quantity of river-fand, to fill up all the interftices: which done, the whole is moiftened, and well rammed again.

Both in their roads and walks, they are very careful to contrive fink-ftones, with proper drains and cefs-pools for carrying off the waters, after violent rains: and to

thofe

thofe that are upon defcents, they never give more fall at the moſt than half an inch to every foot, to prevent their being damaged by the current of the waters.

As China, even in the northern provinces, is exceedingly hot during fummer, much water is employed in their Gardens. In the fmall ones, where the fituation admits, they frequently lay the greateſt part of the ground under water, leaving only fome iflands and rocks; and in their large compofitions, every valley has its brook or rivulet, winding round the feet of the hills, and difcharging themfelves into larger rivers and lakes. Their artiſts aſſert, that no Garden, particularly if it be extenfive, can be perfect, without that element, diftributed in many fhapes; faying, that it is refrefhing and grateful to the fenfe, in the feafons when rural fcenes are moft frequented; that it is a principal fource of variety, from the diverfity of forms and changes of which it is fufceptible; and from the different manners in which it may be combined with other objects; that its impreffions are numerous, and uncommonly forcible; and that, by various modifications,

it

it enables the artist to strengthen the character of every composition; to encrease the tranquility of the quiet scene; to give gloom to the melancholy, gaiety to the pleasing, sublimity to the great, and horror to the terrible.

They observe, that the different aquatic sports of rowing, sailing, swimming, fishing, hunting and combating, are an inexhaustible fund of amusement; that the birds and fishes, inhabitants of the water, are highly entertaining, especially to naturalists; and that the boats and vessels which appear upon its bosom, sometimes furiously impelled by tempests, at others gently gliding over the smooth surface, form, by their combinations, a thousand momentary varied pictures, that animate and embellish every prospect. They compare a clear lake, in a calm sunny day, to a rich piece of painting, upon which the circumambient objects are represented in the highest perfection; and say, it is like an aperture in the world, through which you see another world, another sun, and other skies.

They

They alſo ſay, that the beauty of vegetable nature depends, in a great degree, upon an abundant ſupply of water; which, at the ſame time that it produces variety and contraſt in the ſcenery, enriches the verdure of the lawns, and gives health and vigor to the plantations.

Their lakes are made as large as the ground will admit; ſome ſeveral miles in circumference: and they are ſo ſhaped, that from no ſingle point of view all their terminations can be ſeen; ſo that the ſpectator is always kept in ignorance of their extent. They interſperſe in them many iſlands; which ſerve to give intricacy to the form, to conceal the bounds, and to enrich the ſcenery. Some of theſe are very ſmall, ſufficient only to contain one or two weeping willows, birch, larch, laburnum, or ſome other pendant plants, whoſe branches hang over the water: but others are large, highly cultivated, and enriched with lawns, ſhrubberies, thickets, and buildings: or they are rugged, mountainous, and ſurrounded with rocks and ſhoals; being covered with fern, high graſs, and ſome ſtraggling large trees, planted in the vallies:

amongſt

amongst which are often seen stalking along the elephant, the rhinoceros, the dromedary, the ostrich, and the giant baboon.

There are other islands, raised to a considerable height, by a succession of terraces, communicating to each other by various flights of magnificent steps. At the angles of all these terraces, as well as upon the sides of the steps, are placed many brazen tripods, that smoke with incense; and upon the uppermost platform is generally erected a lofty tower for astronomical observations; an elegant temple, filled with idols; the colossal statue of a god, or some other considerable work; serving, at the same time, as an ornament to the Garden, and as an object to the whole country.

They also introduce in their lakes large artificial rocks, built of a particular fine coloured stone, found on the sea-coasts of China, and designed with much taste. These are pierced with many openings, through which you discover distant prospects; and have in them caverns

for

for the reception of crocodiles, enormous water-ferpents, and other monfters; cages for rare aquatic birds; and grottos, with many fhining apartments, adorned with marine productions, and gems of various forts. They plant upon them all kinds of grafs, creepers and fhrubs which thrive on rocks, fuch as mofs, ground-ivy, fern, ftone-crop, common houfe-leek, and various other forts of the fedum, crane's-bill, dwarf box, rock rofes and broom; with fome trees rooted into the crevices: and they place on their fummits, hermitages and idol temples, to which you afcend by many rugged, winding fteps, cut in the rock.

On the borders of their lakes are feen extenfive galleries, and many detached buildings, of different forms and dimenfions, furrounded with plantations, fea-ports with fleets of veffels lying before them, forts with flags flying, and batteries of cannon; alfo, thickets of flowering fhrubs, meadows covered with cattle, corn lands, cotton and fugar plantations, orchards of various fruit-trees, and rice grounds, which project into the lakes; leaving, in the midft midst of them, passages for boats: and, in some places, the borders consist of lofty woods, with creeks and rivers for the admission of vessels, whose banks are covered with high grass, reeds, and wild spreading trees, forming close gloomy arbors, under which the vessels pass. From these arbors are cut many vistoes through the woods, to distant prospects of towns, bridges, temples, and various other objects, which successively strike the eye, and fill the mind with expectation; when suddenly a farther progress is rendered impracticable, by rocks, strong branches, and whole trees lying cross the channel; between which the river is seen still to continue, with many islands; whereon, and also in the water, appear the remains of antient structures, monumental inscriptions, and fragments of sculpture: which serve to give an edge to curiosity, and to render the disappointment more affecting.

Sometimes too, instead of being intercepted in your passage, the vessel, together with the whole river, are, by the impetuosity and particular direction of the current, hurried into dark caverns, overhung with woods; whence,

whence, after having been furioufly impelled for fome time, you are again difcharged into day-light, upon lakes encompaffed with high hanging woods, rich profpects on mountains, and ftately temples, dedicated to Tien-ho, and the celeftial fpirits.

Upon their lakes, the Chinefe frequently exhibit fea-fights, proceffions, and fhip-races; alfo fire-works and illuminations: in the two laft of which they are more fplendid, and more expert than the Europeans. On fome occafions too, not only the lakes and rivers, but all the pavilions, and every part of their Gardens, are illuminated by an incredible number of beautiful lanterns, of a thoufand different fhapes, intermixed with lampions, torches, fire-pots, and fky-rockets; than which a more magnificent fight cannot be feen. Even the Girandola, and illumination of St. Peter's of the Vatican, though far the moft fplendid exhibitions of that fort in Europe, are trifles, when compared to thefe of China.

Their rivers are feldom ftraight, but winding, and broken into many irregular points: fometimes they are narrow, noisy and rapid; at other times deep, broad and slow. Their banks are variegated, in imitation of nature: being, in some places, bare and gravelly; in others, covered with woods quite to the water's edge; now flat and adorned with flowers and shrubs; then steep, rocky, and forming deep winding caverns, where pigeons of the wood, and water-fowl build their nests; or rising into many little hills, covered with hanging groves; between which are valleys and glades watered by rivulets, and adorned with pleasure-houses, cottages, and rustic temples; with flocks of sheep and goats feeding about them. The terminations of rivers the Chinese artists hide either in woods, or behind hills and buildings; or they turn them under bridges, direct them into caverns, or lose them amongst rocks and shoals.

Both in their lakes and rivers are seen many kinds of reeds, and other aquatic plants and flowers; serving for ornament, as well as for covert to their birds. They erect upon them mills and other hydraulic machines, wherever the situation will permit. They introduce a
great

great many splendid vessels, built after the manner of all nations; and keep in them all kinds of curious and beautiful water-fowl, collected from different countries.

Nor are they less various and magnificent in their bridges than in their other decorations. Some they build of wood, and compose them of rough planks, laid in a rustic manner upon large roots of trees: some are made of many trunks of trees, thrown rudely over the stream; and fenced with decayed branches, intertwined with the convulvulus, and climbers of different sorts: and some are composed of vast arches of carpentry, artfully and neatly framed together. They have also bridges of stone and marble, adorned with colonades, triumphal arches, towers, loggias, fishing pavilions, statues, bas-reliefs, brazen tripods, and porcelain vases. Some of them are upon a curve, or a serpentine plan; others branching out into various directions: some straight, and some at the conflux of rivers or canals, triangular, quadrilateral, and circular, as the situation requires; with pavilions at their angles, and basons of water in their centers, adorned with *Jets d'eau*, and fountains of many sorts.

Some of thefe are entire, and executed with the utmoſt neatneſs and taſte; others ſeem in ruins; and others are left half finiſhed, and ſurrounded with ſcaffolds, machines, and the whole apparatus of building.

It is natural for the reader to imagine, that all theſe bridges, with the pavilions, temples, palaces, and other ſtructures, which have been occaſionally deſcribed in the courſe of this work, and which are ſo abundantly ſcattered over the Chineſe Gardens, ſhould entirely diveſt them of a rural character, and give them rather the appearance of ſplendid cities, than ſcenes of cultivated vegetation. But ſuch is the judgment with which the Chineſe artiſts ſituate their ſtructures, that they enrich and beautify particular proſpects, without any detriment to the general aſpect of the whole compoſition, in which Nature almoſt always appears predominant; for though their Gardens are full of buildings, and other works of art, yet there are many points from which none of them appear: and more than two or three at a time are ſeldom diſcovered; ſo artfully are they concealed in valleys,

behind

behind rocks and mountains, or amongſt woods and thickets.

There are, however, for variety's ſake, in moſt of the Chineſe Gardens, particular places, conſecrated to ſcenes of an extraneous nature; from whence all, or the greateſt part of the buildings are collected into one view, riſing above each other in amphitheatrical order, ſpreading out to a conſiderable extent; and, by their whimſical combinations, exhibiting the moſt magnificent confuſion imaginable. Their artiſts knowing how powerfully contraſt agitates the human mind, loſe no opportunity of practiſing ſudden tranſitions, or of diſplaying ſtrong oppoſitions, as well in the nature of the objects which enter into their compoſitions, as in their modifications. Thus they conduct you from limited proſpects to extenſive views; from places of horror to ſcenes of delight; from lakes and rivers to woods and lawns; and from the ſimpleſt arrangements of nature, to the moſt complicated productions of art. To dull and gloomy colours, they oppoſe ſuch as are brilliant; and to light, they oppoſe darkneſs: rendering, by thefe means, their productions not only diftinct in the parts, but alfo uncommonly ftriking in their total effect.

The cafcades of the Chinefe, which are always introduced, where the ground admits, and where the fupply of water is fufficient, are fometimes regular, like thofe of Marli, Frefcati and Tivoli; but more frequently they are rude, like the falls of Trolhetta and the Nile. In one place a whole river is precipitated from the fummit of the mountain, into the vallies beneath; where it foams and whirls amongft the rocks, till it falls down other precipices, and buries itfelf in the gloom of impenetrable forefts. In another place the waters burft out with violence from many parts, fpouting a great number of cafcades, in different directions; which, through various impediments, at laft unite, and form one great expanfe of water. Sometimes the view of the cafcade is in a great meafure intercepted by the branches which hang over it; fometimes its paffage is obftructed by trees, and heaps of enormous ftones, that feem to have been brought down by the fury of the torrent: and frequently

rough

rough wooden bridges are thrown from one rock to another, over the steepest parts of the cataract; narrow winding paths are carried along the edges of the precipices; and mills and huts are suspended over the waters; the seeming dangerous situation of which, adds to the horror of the scene.

As the Chinese are so very fond of water, their Gardeners endeavour to obtain it by art, wherever it is denied by Nature. For this purpose, they have many ingenious inventions to collect water; and many machines, of simple construction, which raise it to almost any level, at a trifling expence. They use the same method for overflowing vallies, that is practised in Europe; by raising heads of earth or masonry at their extremities: where the soil is too porous to hold water, they clay the bottom, in the same manner that we do to make it tight: and in order to prevent the inconveniences arising from stagnant waters, they always contrive a considerable discharge to procure motion, even where the supply is scanty; which is done by conveying the discharged water back, through subterraneous

raneous drains, into refervoirs; whence it is again raifed into the lake or river, by means of pumps, and other machines, proper for that purpofe. They always give a confiderable depth to their waters, at leaft five or fix feet, to prevent the rifing of fcum, and the floating of weeds upon the furface; and they are always provided with fwans, and fuch other birds as feed on weeds, to keep them under.

In overflowing their grounds, and alfo in draining them, they take all poffible care not to kill many of their old trees, either by over moiftening their roots, or draining them too much; faying, that the lofs of a fine old plant is irreparable; that it impairs the beauty of the adjacent plantations; and often likewife deftroys the effect of the fcenery, from many diftant points of view: and in fhaping their grounds, they are, for the fame reafon, equally cautious with regard to the old plantations; carefully obferving never to bury the ftems, nor to expofe the roots of any trees which they mean to preferve.

In their plantations, the Chinese artists do not, as is the practice of some European Gardeners, plant indiscriminately every thing that comes in their way; nor do they ignorantly imagine that the whole perfection of plantations consists in the variety of the trees and shrubs of which they are composed: on the contrary, their practice is guided by many rules, founded on reason and long observation, from which they seldom or ever deviate.

" Many trees, shrubs and flowers," sayeth Li-Tsong, a Chinese author of great antiquity, " thrive best in low
" moist situations; many on hills and mountains: some
" require a rich soil; but others will grow on clay, in
" sand, or even upon rocks; and in the water: to
" some a sunny exposition is necessary; but for others,
" the shade is preferable. There are plants which thrive
" best in exposed situations; but, in general, shelter is
" requisite. The skilful Gardener, to whom study and
" experience have taught these qualities, carefully attends
" to them in his operations; knowing that thereon de-

" pend the health and growth of his plants; and con-
" fequently the beauty of his plantations."

In China, as in Europe, the ufual times of planting are the autumn and the fpring; fome things anfwering beft when planted in the firft, and fome in the laft of thefe feafons. Their Gardeners avoid planting, whenever the grounds are fo moift as to endanger the rotting of the roots; or when the frofts are fo near as to pinch the plants, before they have recovered the fhock of tranf-plantation; or when the earth and air are too dry to afford nurture to them; or when the weather is fo tempeftuous as to fhake or overturn them, whilft loofe and unrooted in the ground.

They obferve, that the perfection of trees for Ornamental Gardening, confifts in their fize; in the beauty and variety of their forms; in the colour and fmoothnefs of their bark; in the quantity, fhape, and rich verdure of their foliage; in its early appearance in the fpring, and long duration in the autumn; in the quicknefs of their growth;

growth; in their hardinefs to endure the extremities of heat, cold, drought and moifture; in their making no litter, during the fpring or fummer, by the fall of the bloffom; and in the ftrength of their branches, to refift, unhurt, the violence of tempefts.

They fay, that the perfection of fhrubs confifts not only in moft of the above mentioned particulars, but alfo in the beauty, durability, or long fucceffion of their bloffom; and in their fair appearance before the bloom, and after it is gone.

" We are fenfible," fay they, " that no plant is pof-
" feffed of all good qualities; but choofe fuch as have
" the feweft faults; and avoid all the exotics, that vege-
" tate with difficulty in our climate; for though they
" may be rare, they cannot be beautiful, being always
" in a fickly ftate: have, if you pleafe, hot-houfes and
" cool-houfes, for plants of every region, to fatisfy the
" curiofity of botanifts; but they are mere infirmaries:
" the plants which they contain, are valetudinarians, di-
" vefted

"vested of beauty and vigor; which only exist by the power of medicine, and by dint of good nursing."

The excessive variety of which some European Gardeners are so fond in their plantations, the Chinese artists blame, observing, that a great diversity of colours, foliage, and direction of branches, must create confusion, and destroy all the masses upon which effect and grandeur depend: they observe too, that it is unnatural; for, as in Nature most plants sow their own seeds, whole forests are generally composed of the same sort of trees. They admit, however, of a moderate variety; but are by no means promiscuous in the choice of their plants; attending, with great care, to the colour, form, and foliage of each; and only mixing together such as harmonize and assemble agreeably.

They say that some trees are only proper for thickets; others only fit to be employed singly; and others equally adapted to both these situations. The mountain-cedar, the spruce and silver firs, and all others whose branches have

have an horizontal direction, they hold improper for thickets; becaufe their branches indent into each other; and likewife cut difagreeably upon the plants which back them. They never mix thefe horizontal branched trees with the cyprefs, the oriental arbor vitæ, or other upright ones; nor with the larix, the weeping willow, the birch, the laburnum, or others of a pendant nature; faying, that the interfection of their branches forms a very unpicturefque kind of net-work: neither do they employ together the catalpha and the acacia, the yew and the willow, the plane and the fhumach, nor any of fuch heterogeneous forts; but on the contrary, they affemble in their large woods, the oak, the elm, the beech, the tulip, the fycamore, maple and plane, the Indian chefnut and weftern walnut, the arbeal, the lime, and all whofe luxuriant foliages hide the direction of their branches; and growing in globular maffes, affemble well together; forming, by the harmonious combination of their tints, one grand mafs of rich verdure.

In their fmaller plantations, they employ trees of a fmaller growth, but of the fame concordant forts; bordering them with Perſian lilacks, gelder-roſes, ſeringas, coronillas or ſennas of various ſorts, flowering raſberries, yellow jeſſamine, hypericum or St. John's wort, the ſpiræa frutex, altheas, roſes, and other flowering ſhrubs; intermixed with flowers and with the padus of various ſpecies, elder, mountain aſh, acacia, double bloſſomed thorn, and many other ſorts of flowering trees: and wherever the ground is bare, they cover it with white, blue, purple and variegated periwinkle, the convulvulus minor, dwarf ſtocks, violets, primroſes, and different kinds of creeping flowers ; and with ſtrawberries, tutſen and ivy, which climbs up and covers the ſtems of the trees.

In their ſhrubberies they follow, as much as poſſible, the ſame rules; obſerving farther, in ſome of them to plant all ſuch ſhrubs as flouriſh at one time; and in others, ſuch as ſucceed each other : of which different methods the firſt is much the moſt brilliant; but its duration is ſhort ; and the appearance of the ſhrubbery is generally ſhabby, as ſoon as the bloom is off : they therefore ſeldom uſe it, but for ſcenes that are to be enjoyed at certain periods ;

periods; preferring the laft, on other occafions, as being of long duration, and lefs unpleafing after the flowers are gone.

The Chinefe Gardeners do not fcatter their flowers indifcriminately about their borders, as is ufual in fome parts of Europe, but difpofe them with great circumfpection; and, if I may be allowed the expreffion, paint their way very artfully along the fkirts of the plantations: and in other places, where flowers are to be introduced. They reject all that are of a ftraggling growth, of harfh colours, and poor foliage; choofing only fuch as are of fome duration, grow either large, or in clufters, are of beautiful forms, well leaved, and of tints that harmonize with the greens that furround them. They avoid all fudden tranfitions, both with regard to dimenfion and colour; rifing gradually from the fmalleft flowers to hollioaks, pœonies, fun-flowers, carnations, poppies, and others of the boldeft growth; and varying their tints, by eafy gradations, from white, ftraw colour, purple and incarnate, to the deepeft blues, and moft brilliant crimfons

and

and scarlets. They frequently blend several roots together, whose leaves and flowers unite, and compose only one rich harmonious mass; such as the white and purple candituff, larkspurs, and mallows of various colours, double poppies, loopins, primroses, pinks and carnations; with many others, whose forms and colours accord with each other: and the same method they use with flowering shrubs; blending white, red, and variegated roses together; purple and white lilacks; yellow and white jessamine; altheas of various sorts; and as many others, as they can with any propriety unite.---By these mixtures they encrease considerably the variety and beauty of their compositions.

In their large plantations, the flowers generally grow in the natural ground: but in their flower-gardens, and in all other parts that are highly kept, they are in pots, buried in the ground; which, as fast as the bloom goes off, are removed, and others are brought in their places; so that there is a constant succession, for almost every month in the year; and the flowers are never seen, but in the height of their beauty.

Amongst the most interesting parts of the Chinese plantations, are their open groves; for as the women spend much of their time there, care is taken to situate them as pleasantly as possible, and to adorn them with all kinds of natural beauties.

The ground on which they are planted, is commonly uneven, yet not rugged; either on a plain, raised into many gentle swellings; on the easy declivity of a mountain, commanding rich prospects; or in vales, surrounded with woods, and watered with springs and rivulets.

Those which are in an open exposure, are generally bordered with flowery meadows, extensive corn-fields, or large lakes; the Chinese artists observing, that the brilliancy and gaiety of these objects, form a pleasing contrast with the gloom of the grove: and when they are confined in thickets, or close planted woods, the plantation is so formed that, from every approach, some part of the grove is hid; which opening gradually to the eye of the passenger, satisfies his curiosity by degrees.

Some of thefe groves are compofed of evergreens, chiefly of pyramidal forms, thinly planted over the furface, with flowering fhrubs fcattered amongft them: others are compofed of lofty fpreading trees, whofe foliage affords a fhady retreat during the heat of the day. The plants are never crowded together; fufficient room being left between them for fitting or walking upon the grafs; which, by reafon of its fhady fituation, retains a conftant verdure; and, in the fpring, is adorned with a great variety of early flowers, fuch as violets, crocus's, polianthus's and primrofes; hyacinths, cowflips, fnow-drops, daffodils and daifies. Some trees of the grove are fuffered to branch out from the very bottom of the ftem upwards; others, for the fake of variety, have their ftems bare: but far the greater number are furrounded with rofe-trees, fweet-briar, honeyfuckles, fcarlet beans, nafturtiums, everlafting and fweet-fcented peas, double-bloffomed briar, and other odoriferous fhrubs, which beautify the barren parts of the plant, and perfume the air.

Sometimes too their open groves are compofed of lemon, orange, citron, pompelmofe, and myrtle-trees; which, as the climate varies, either grow in the earth, or in buried tubs and pots, which are removed to green houses during the winter. They also have groves of all sorts of fine formed fruit-trees; which, when they bloſſom, and also when their fruit is ripe, are exceedingly beautiful: and to add to the luxuriance of theſe ſcenes, the Chineſe artiſts plant vines of different coloured grapes near many of the trees, which climb up their ſtems, and afterwards hang in feſtoons from one tree to another.

In all their open groves are kept young broods of pheaſants, partridges, pea-fowls, turkies, and all kinds of handſome domeſtic birds, who flock thither, at certain times of the day, to be fed: they alſo retain in them, by the ſame method, ſquirrels, ſmall monkies, crocatoos, parrots, hog deer, ſpotted capritos, lambs, Guinea pigs, and many other little beautiful birds and animals.

The trees which the Chineſe Gardeners uſe in their open groves, and also for detached trees, or groupes of two, three, or four together, are the mountain cedar, the

ſpruce

spruce silver and balm of Gilead firs, the larix, the smooth stemmed or Weymouth pine, the arbor vitæ, and cypress; the weeping willow, the ash, the maple, western walnut, arbeal, tulip, acacia, oak, elm, and all others that grow in picturesque forms: and whenever they loose their natural shape, either by too quick vegetation, or other accidents, they endeavour to reduce them to an agreeable form, by lopping off their exuberances; or by forcing them into other directions. The Indian, or horse-chesnut, the lime, and some others of a stiff, formal growth, they never use detached; but find them, on account of their rich verdure, their blossom, and abundant foliage, very fit for thickets, woods and avenues.

They have particular plants for the dressed gay parts of the Garden; others in their wilds and scenes of horror; and others appropriated to monuments and ruins; or to accompany buildings of various sorts; according as their properties fit them for these different purposes.

In planting, they are nicely attentive to the natural size of their plants; placing such as are of humble growth in the front; and those that are higher, gradually inwards: that all may be exposed to view at the same time. They appropriate certain plants to low moist situations; and others to those that are dry and lofty; strictly attending therein to Nature: for though a willow, say they, may grow upon a mountain, or an oak in a bog, yet are not these by any means natural situations for either.

When the patron is rich, they consider nothing but perfection in their plantations: but when he is poor, they have also an eye to œconomy; introducing such plants, trees and buildings, into their design, as are not only beautiful, but also useful. Instead of lawns, they have meadows and fields, covered with sheep and other cattle; or lands planted with rice and cotton, or sowed with corn, turneps, beans, pease, hemp, and other things that produce flowers, and variegated pieces of colouring. The groves are composed of all useful kinds of fruit-trees; such as apple, pear, cherry, mulberry, plumb, apricot, fig, olive, filbert, and many others, peculiar to China.

The woods are full of timber-trees, useful for fuel and building; which also produce chesnuts, walnuts, acorns, and other profitable fruits and seeds: and both woods and groves abound with game of all sorts.

The shrubberies consist of rose, rasberry, bramble, currant, lavender, vine and goosberry bushes; with barberry, alder, peach, nectarine and almond trees. All the walks are narrow, and carried under the drip of the trees, and skirts of the plantation, that they may occupy no useful ground: and of the buildings, some are barns for grain or hay; some stables for horses and oxen; some dairies, with their cow-houses and calf-pens; some cottages for the husbandmen, with sheds for implements of husbandry; some are dove-houses; others menageries for breeding poultry; and others stoves and green-houses, for raising early or rare fruits, vegetables and flowers: all judiciously placed, and designed with taste, though in a rustic style.

The lakes and rivers are well stored with fish and water-fowl: and all the vessels contrived for fishing,

hunting,

hunting, and other sports that are profitable as well as entertaining. In their borders they plant, instead of flowers, sweet herbs, celery, carrots, potatoes, strawberries, scarlet beans, nasturtiums, endive, cucumbers, melons, pineapples, and other handsome fruits and vegetables: and all the less sightly productions for the kitchen, are carefully hid behind espaliers of fruit-trees.---Thus, they say, that every farmer may have a Garden without expence; and that if all land-holders were men of taste, the world might be formed into one continued Garden, without difficulty.

Such is the substance of what I have hitherto collected relative to the Gardens of the Chinese. My endeavour, in the present Publication, has been to give the general outline of their style of Gardening, without entering into trifling particulars, and without enumerating many little rules of which their artists occasionally avail themselves; being persuaded that, to men of genius, such minute discriminations are always unnecessary, and often prejudicial, as they burden the memory, and clog the imagination with superfluous restrictions.

The difpofitions and different artifices mentioned in the preceding pages, are thofe which are chiefly practifed in China, and fuch as beft characterize their ftyle of Gardening. But the artifts of that country are fo inventive, and fo various in their combinations, that no two of their compofitions are ever alike : they never copy nor imitate each other; they do not even repeat their own productions; faying, that what has once been feen, operates feebly at a fecond infpection; and that whatever bears even a diftant refemblance to a known object, feldom excites a new idea. The reader is therefore not to imagine that what has been related is all that exifts; on the contrary, a confiderable number of other examples might have been produced : but thofe that have been offered, will probably be fufficient; more efpecially as moft of them are like certain compofitions in mufick, which, though fimple in themfelves, fuggeft, to a fertile imagination, an endlefs fucceffion of complicated variations.

To the generality of Europeans many of the foregoing
defcriptions

descriptions may seem improbable; and the execution of what has been described, in some measure impracticable: but those who are better acquainted with the East, know that nothing is too great for Eastern magnificence to attempt; and there can be few impossibilities, where treasures are inexhaustible, where power is unlimited, and where munificence has no bounds.

European artists must not hope to rival Oriental splendor; yet let them look up to the sun, and copy as much of its lustre as they can, circumstances will frequently obstruct them in their course, and they may often be prevented from soaring high: but their attention should constantly be fixed on great objects; and their productions always demonstrate, that they knew the road to perfection, had they been enabled to proceed on the journey.

Where twining serpentine walks, scattering shrubs, digging holes to raise mole-hills, and ringing never-ceasing changes on lawns, groves and thickets, is called Gardening, it matters little who are the Gardeners; whether a peasant or a Pouffin; whether a child in fport, or a man for hire: the meaneft may do the little there is to be done, and the beft could reach no farther. But wherever a better ftyle is adopted, and Gardens are to be natural, without refemblance to vulgar Nature; new without affectation, and extraordinary without extravagance; where the fpectator is to be amufed, where his attention is conftantly to be kept up, his curiofity excited, and his mind agitated by a great variety of oppofite paffions; there Gardeners muft be men of genius, experience and judgement; quick in perception, rich in expedients, fertile in imagination, and thoroughly verfed in all the affections of the human mind.

F I N I S.

ERRATA.

Page 40, line 17, *for* camufath fkin, *read* camufathkin.

Page 66, line 5, *for* to, *read* with.

Page 81, line 11, *for* fhumach, *read* fumach.

Page 83, line 17, *for* carnations, poppies, *read* carnation-poppies.

Page 87, line 14, *for* crocatoos, *read* cokatoos.

www.ingramcontent.com/pod-product-compliance
Lightning Source LLC
Chambersburg PA
CBHW032242080426
42735CB00008B/961